LIFE, BY HIS DEATH!

LIFE, BY HIS DEATH!

An easier-to-read and abridged version of the classic
"The Death of Death in the Death of Christ",
by Dr. John Owen, 1616–1683

Prepared by H. J. Appleby

Foreword by J. I. Packer, M.A., D.Phil.

General Editor—J. K. Davies, B.D.

© Grace Publications Trust
139 Grosvenor Avenue
LONDON N5 2NH
England
1992

Joint Managing Editors:
J P Arthur MA
H J Appleby

Printed 1981, 1992, 1997

We gratefully acknowledge the help and encouragement
received from the Banner of Truth Trust (3 Murrayfield Road,
Edinburgh, EH12 6EL), the publishers of the full version of
"The Death of Death in the Death of Christ" from whom it is
available.

ISBN 0 9505476 3 8

Distributed by:
EVANGELICAL PRESS
Grange Close,
Faverdale Industrial Estate
Darlington
DL3 0PH
England

Cover design: Lawrence Littleton Evans

Printed and bound by Cox & Wyman Ltd, Reading, Berkshire

CONTENTS

FOREWORD

Extract from the Introductory Essay by Dr. J. I. Packer to "The Death of Death in the Death of Christ" by Dr. J. Owen, in the Banner of Truth Trust edition, 1959.

"*The Death of Death in the Death of Christ* is a polemical work, designed to show, among other things, that the doctrine of universal redemption is unscriptural and destructive of the gospel. There are many, therefore, to whom it is not likely to be of interest. Those who see no need for doctrinal exactness and have no time for theological debates which show up divisions between so-called Evangelicals may well regret its reappearance. Some may find the very sound of Owen's thesis so shocking that they will refuse to read his book at all; so passionate a thing is prejudice, and so proud are we of our theological shibboleths. But it is hoped that this reprint will find itself readers of a different spirit. There are signs today of a new upsurge of interest in the theology of the Bible: a new readiness to test traditions, to search the Scriptures and to think through the faith. It is to those who share this readiness that Owen's treatise is offered, in the belief that it will help us in one of the most urgent tasks facing Evangelical Christendom today – the recovery of the gospel.

"This last remark may cause some raising of eyebrows, but it seems to be warranted by the facts.

"There is no doubt that Evangelicalism today is in a state of perplexity and unsettlement. In such matters as the practice of evangelism, the teaching of holiness, the building up of local church life, the pastor's dealing with souls and the exercise of discipline, there is evidence of widespread dissatisfaction with things as they are and of equally widespread uncertainty as to the road ahead. This is a complex phenomenon, to which many factors have contributed; but, if we go to the root of the matter, we shall find that these perplexities are all ultimately due to our having lost our grip on the biblical gospel. Without realising it, we have during the past century bartered that gospel for a substitute product which, though it looks similar enough in points of detail, is as a whole a decidedly different thing. Hence our troubles; for the substitute product does not answer the ends for which the authentic gospel has in past days proved itself so mighty. The new gospel conspicuously fails to produce deep reverence, deep repentance, deep humility, a spirit of worship, a concern for the church. Why? We would suggest that the reason lies in its own character and content. It fails to make men God-centred in their thoughts and God-fearing in their hearts, because this is not primarily what it is trying to do. One way of stating the difference between it and the old gospel is to say that it is too exclusively concerned to be 'helpful' to man – to bring peace, comfort, happiness, satisfaction – and too little concerned to glorify God. The old gospel was 'helpful', too – more so, indeed, than is the new – but (so to speak) incidentally, for its first concern was always to give glory to God. It was always and essentially a proclamation of Divine sovereignty in mercy and judgment, a summons to bow down and worship the mighty Lord on whom man depends for all good, both in nature and in grace. Its centre of reference was unambiguously God. But in the new gospel the centre of reference is man. This is just to say that the old gospel was *religious* in a way that the new gospel is not. Whereas the chief aim of the old was to teach men to worship God, the concern of the new seems limited to making them feel better. The subject of the old gospel was God and His ways with men; the subject of the new is man and the help God gives him. There is a world of difference. The whole perspective and emphasis of gospel preaching has changed.

"From this change of interest has sprung a change of content, for the new gospel has in effect reformulated the biblical message in the supposed interests of 'helpfulness'. Accordingly, the themes of man's natural inability to believe, of God's free election being the ultimate cause of salvation, and of Christ dying specifically for His sheep, are not preached. These doctrines, it would be said, are not 'helpful'; they would drive sinners to despair, by suggesting to them that it is not in their own power to be saved through Christ. (The possibility that such despair might be salutary is not considered; it is taken for granted that it cannot be, because it is so shattering to our self-esteem.) However this may be, the result of these omissions is that part of the biblical gospel is now preached as if it were the whole of that gospel; and a half-truth masquerading as the whole truth becomes a compete untruth. Thus, we appeal to men as if they all had the ability to receive Christ at any time; we speak of His redeeming work as if He had done no more by dying than make it possible for us to save ourselves by believing; we speak of God's love as if it were no more than a general willingness to receive any who will turn and trust; and we depict the Father and the Son, not as sovereignly active in drawing sinners to themselves, but as waiting in quiet impotence 'at the door of our hearts' for us to let them in. It is undeniable that this is how we preach; perhaps this is what we really believe. But it needs to be said with emphasis that this set of twisted half-truths is something other than the biblical gospel. The Bible is against us when we preach in this way; and the fact that such preaching has become almost standard practice among us only shows how urgent it is that we should review this matter. To recover the old, authentic, biblical gospel, and to bring our preaching and practice back into line with it, is perhaps our most pressing present need. And it is at this point that Owen's treatise on redemption can give us help."

PREFACE

Why this book was written

Let me explain why I have written this book. I am the last person to enjoy controversy! But the Bible says we must "contend earnestly for the faith once delivered to the saints". In recent years I have frequently been consulted about the subject of this book. And I hear that these matters are being debated in all parts of the country. So I was convinced that such a book should be written. I had rather the work was done by someone else; but I felt it better to be done by me than not done at all!

I do not claim to be the best person to write such a book as this. Others have written well on the same subject. Yet I notice that they limit themselves to certain points of the controversy. And I thought it would be better not merely to say what Christ did not do by his death, but also to explain fully what he did do.

For seven years I have studied this subject, both in the Bible, and in all other available books. Can I suggest therefore that you now read my book carefully? If anyone wishes to disprove individual points taken out of the context of this book, they have my permission to enjoy their imaginary success. But if anyone seriously studies the whole book, then I think they must be convinced by it.

I hope the book gives satisfaction to those who know these truths, strength to those who are weak in them, and

above all, glory to the Lord whose truths they are, though
I am his most unworthy labourer.

JOHN OWEN
1648

INTRODUCTION

What this book is about

The Bible says that the death of Jesus Christ was like a payment to set men free from sin. So far so good; but now there is a problem! Did Christ's death free all men, or only some men, from their sin? Christians are divided in their views. Some say one thing, some say the other. So what does the Bible say? That is what we need to find out.

If we say Christ's death was for everyone, then we cannot at the same time say it was only for those people whom God had chosen. If Christ died for everyone, God had no need to choose a special people, had he? On the other hand, if we say that God did choose a special people – as the Bible teaches – then it would have been pointless for Christ to die for everyone, wouldn't it?

If we say Christ's death was a ransom, or payment, for all the human race, then, either:

1. all men must have the power to accept or reject that ransom for themselves; or:
2. all men must actually be ransomed by Christ, whether they know it or not.

Christ's death for all men could only be realistic, if one of these statements is true. But the first suggestion denies the Bible teaching that men are helplessly dead in sin and in themselves have no power to come to Christ. The second suggestion denies the Bible teaching that some men are lost for ever. Obviously, there are grave difficulties about suggesting that Christ's death was for all men.

Why is it, then, that some people say that Christ's death was for everyone? There seem to be five possible reasons:

1. It seems to make God more "attractive", if they say Christ's death was for everyone.
2. It seems to make God's love "greater", if they say he loves all men equally.
3. It seems to make Christ's death more "valuable", if they can say that it was a payment for the sins of everyone.
4. The Bible seems to use the words "all" and "the world" as though they mean "everyone".
5. Some may just want to say Christ's death was for everyone, so that they can be included, although they do not want to change the ungodly way they are living!

In this book:

We are going to see why these five reasons are wrong, and what the Bible does teach about the purpose of the death of Jesus Christ.

PART ONE

God's purpose in sending Jesus Christ to die

(Part Two studies in detail what Christ actually achieved by his death)

CHAPTER ONE

Introducing the problem

Christ himself told us why he came into the world. He said: "The Son of Man came to seek and to save what was lost" (Luke 19:10). On another occasion, he said the Son of Man had come "to give his life a ransom for many" (Mark 10:45).

The Apostle Paul also clearly stated why Christ came into the world: "The Lord Jesus Christ who gave himself for our sins to rescue us from the present evil age" (Galatians 1:4). "Christ Jesus came into the world to save sinners" (I Timothy 1:15). "Jesus Christ, who gave himself for us, to redeem us from all wickedness, and to purify for himself a people that are his very own, eager to do what is good" (Titus 2:14).

From these statements, it is clear that the purpose of Christ's death was:

> to save people from sin,
> to deliver people from this evil world,
> to make people pure and holy,
> to create people who do good works.

Other Bible passages explain what Jesus Christ actually did in his death. There are five things we can notice:

1. People are reconciled to God by it (Romans 5:1).
2. People are forgiven and justified by it (Romans 3:24).
3. People are made clean and holy by it (Hebrews 9:14).

4. People are adopted as God's sons by it (Galatians 4:4, 5).
5. People receive glory and everlasting life (Hebrews 9:15).

From all this evidence, the Bible's teaching is clear: the death of Christ was intended to bring to men (and actually does so) forgiveness now, and glory to come. If, therefore, Christ died for all men, then either:

all men are now freed from sin, and they are forgiven and will be glorified, or:

Christ has failed in his purpose.

The first of these we know to be untrue by our daily experience of men. The second suggestion – that Christ failed – is an insult to God.

To escape from the problem of accepting one or other of these two suggestions, those who say Christ did die for all men say it was not God's purpose for all men to benefit. They say the benefit is only for those who produce a faith to believe in Christ. This act of faith must be something that some men do on their own, making them different from other men. (If faith was something obtained by Christ's death, and if he died for all men, then all men would have faith!) Such a suggestion as this seems to me to make smaller what Christ actually obtained by his death, so I shall oppose it by showing that what the Bible teaches is quite different!

CHAPTER TWO

The Who, How and What of a thing

There are three words we shall use a lot in this book, and it will help to introduce them briefly now. When any action takes place, there is an *agent* (*who* does it); there are *means* used (*how* it is done); and there is an *end* in view (the *what*, or end result).

We choose *how* we'll do a thing (the means) according to *what* it is we want to do (the end). So we can say that the *end* is the *reason* for the *means*. And if we have chosen the right *means*, the *end* is certain. So we can say the *means* is the *cause* of the *end*. Clearly, if the *agent* intending to do something has chosen the right *means* to do it, then it cannot fail to be done!

Now we can apply these principles to our discussion in this book. We shall first see who the *agent* is who intends to redeem us. Then we shall see what means were used to redeem us. And finally (in Part Two) we shall see what was the *result* of the *means* used.

According to the Bible, the *agent* intending our salvation is the Triune God. All other *agencies* were merely *instruments* in his hand (Acts 4:28). The chief agent is the Holy Trinity. Let's study this in more detail ...

CHAPTER THREE

God the Father, Agent of our salvation

To the question, How was God the Father the agent of our salvation? I answer: There are two ways: it was the Father who sent the Son to die, and it was the Father who punished Christ for our sins. We can examine these two things in more detail.

1. It is clear from many Bible verses that the Father sent the Son into the world. For example: "when the time was fully come, God sent his Son, born of a woman, born under law, to redeem those under the law, that we might receive the full rights of sons" (Galatians 4:4–5). This sending of the Son involved God the Father in three things:
    i.   there was the original purpose that had always been in his mind (I Peter 1:20).
    ii. there was his act of giving the Son all the abilities he needed to do the work he was sent to do (John 3:34, 35).*
    iii. and there was his act of promising his Son all the help he needed for success in the work (Acts 4:10, 11).

2. It is clear from many Bible verses that the Father punished Jesus Christ for our sins. For example: "God made him who knew no sin to be sin on our behalf, that we might become the righteousness of God in him" (II Corinthians 5:21). It can be said that Christ suffered and died *instead of us*. That being so, isn't it a strange idea that Christ should

* As the Son of God, he already had the perfection of Deity; but as the Son of Man he had to be given the gifts he needed.

6

suffer instead of those who will also suffer for their own sins themselves?

We can put the matter like this: Christ suffered for either,

> all the sins of all men, or
> all the sins of some men, or
> some of the sins of all men.

If the last statement is true, then all men are still left with some sins, and so no-one can be redeemed.

If the first statement is true, then why are not all men freed from sin? You may say, Because of their unbelief. But I ask, Is unbelief a sin? If it is not, why are men punished for it? If it is a sin, then it must be among the sins for which Christ died. So the first statement cannot be true!

So it is clear that the only possibility remaining is that Christ had laid upon him all the sins of some men, the elect, only. It is this that I believe is the teaching of the Bible.

(Part Four of this book deals with passages of scripture using the words "world" and "all".)

CHAPTER FOUR

God the Son, Agent of our salvation

Because God the Son willingly agreed to do what the Father had planned, we can say that he too was an agent of our salvation. Jesus said: "My food is to do the will of him who sent me, and to accomplish his work" (John

4:34). There are three ways in which Christ showed his willingness to be an agent:

1. He was willing to lay aside the glory of his divine nature, and appear as a man. "Since the children share in flesh and blood, he himself likewise also partook of the same" (Hebrews 2:14). Notice that it is said that he did this, not because the whole human race was composed of flesh and blood, but because "the children whom God had given him" (Hebrews 2:13) were human. His willingness was related to those children, not to the whole human race.

2. He was willing to give himself as an offering. It is true that he suffered many things passively. Yet it is also true that he gave himself to those sufferings actively and willingly. Without such willing consent, the sufferings would not have had any value. So he could truthfully say: "The Father loves me, because I lay down my life ... no-one takes it away from me, but I lay it down of my own accord" (John 10:17, 18).

3. His present prayers for his children show his willingness to be an agent in their salvation. Christ has now entered into the heavenly holy place (Hebrews 9:11–12). His work there is intercession (prayer). Notice that he does not pray for the world (John 17:9), but for those for whom he died (Romans 8:34). He asks that those who have been given to him shall come where he is, to see his glory (John 17:24). So it is clear that he could not have died for all men!

CHAPTER FIVE

God the Spirit, Agent of our salvation

The Bible speaks of three things in which the Holy Spirit works with the Father and the Son in redeeming us. And these activities show him to be an agent of our salvation too.

1. The human body which the Son took, when he became a man, was created by the Holy Spirit, within Mary. "She was found to be with child through the Holy Spirit" (Matthew 1:18).

2. The Bible says that when the Son offered himself as a sacrifice, he did so by the Spirit. "Who, through the eternal Spirit offered himself unblemished to God" (Hebrews 9:14). From this, it is clear that the Holy Spirit was in some way the instrument that made the offering possible.

3. There are clear Bible statements showing that the work of raising Christ from the dead was the work of the Holy Spirit. "He was put to death in the body but made alive by the Spirit" (I Peter 3:18).

Clearly, the Holy Spirit had important things to do, joining with the Father and the Son in their purpose of redeeming us.

We have seen that each Person of the Trinity can be called an agent of our salvation. It is important to remember, however, that although for the purpose of our study, we have distinguished between the work of each of the divine Persons, there are not in fact three agents of our salvation, but one, for God is One. So we can say that the whole Trinity is the agent of our redemption.

CHAPTER SIX

The work of Christ is the means used to obtain our salvation

As we saw in Chapter Two, the agent who does a thing uses certain means to reach the particular end he has in view. And in the actual work of our salvation, there are two actions that Christ has done. (I am not thinking here of the eternal planning to make our salvation possible, but only of the producing of it in historical times.) These two historical acts of Christ are:

1. His offering of himself in the past, and
2. His intercession for us now.

In Christ's offering of himself, I include his willingness to suffer all that was involved in his coming to die: his emptying of himself of his glory, and being born of a woman; his acts of humility and obedience to the Father's will throughout his life; and, finally, there was his death on the cross.

And in Christ's intercession for us, I include also his resurrection and ascension, for these are the basis of his intercession. Without them, no intercession would be possible.

We shall look at these two things in more detail in the next chapter, but I want to make some comments now. Both of these acts have *the same intention*. The offering and the intercession are each in order "to bring many sons to glory" (Hebrews 2:10). The benefits intended by both these acts are for *the same people*; he prays for those for whom he died (John 17:9). We know that his intercession must be successful – "I know that thou hearest me always", he once said (John 11:41). It follows then that

10

all for whom he died must receive all the good things obtained by that death. That clearly destroys the teaching that Christ died for all men!

CHAPTER SEVEN

Christ's offering of himself and his intercession are the one means to accomplish our redemption

It is important to notice how, in the scriptures, Christ's offering of himself and his intercession are linked together. For example:

Christ justifies those whose iniquities (or sins) he carried. (Isaiah 53:11)

Christ intercedes for those whose sins he carried. (Isaiah 53:12)

Christ rose from the dead to justify those for whom he died. (Romans 4:25)

Christ died for God's elect and now prays for them. (Romans 8:33-34)

From this it is clear that Christ cannot have died for all men; for if he had, then all men would be justified – which, clearly, they are not.

To sacrifice and to pray are both duties required of a priest. If he fails in either, he fails to be a faithful priest for his people. Jesus Christ is spoken of both as our propitiation (sacrifice) and as our advocate (representative) (I John 2:1-2). He is spoken of both as offering his blood (Hebrews 9:11-14), and as interceding for us (Hebrews 7:25). Because he is a faithful priest, he must

11

perform both these duties perfectly. Since his prayers are always heard, he cannot be interceding for all men, for all men are not saved. From this, it must be clear that he could not have died for all men either.

We should also remember the way in which Christ now intercedes for us. Scripture says that it is by his presenting his blood in heaven (Hebrews 9:11, 12, 24). In other words, he intercedes by presenting his sufferings to the Father. The two acts, suffering and intercession, must therefore relate to the same persons, or it would be pointless to use the one as the basis for the other.

Christ himself joins together his death and his intercession, as the one means of our redemption, in his prayer in John chapter 17. In this prayer he refers to his giving himself in death, and his praying for his own whom the Father had given him. We may not separate these two acts, if Christ himself joins them. One, without the other, would be useless anyway, as Paul argues: "If Christ has not been raised (and therefore is not now interceding) your faith is worthless; you are still in your sins". (I Corinthians 15:17).

So there is no assurance of salvation for us, if we separate Christ's death from his intercession. What good would it be to say that Christ died for me, in the past, if he does not *now* intercede for me? Only if he now justifies us are we safe from the condemnation of our sins. I could still be condemned if Christ does not plead for me. So it is clear that his intercession must be for the same people as those for whom he died – and therefore he cannot have died for all!

PART TWO

*The true purpose of the death of Christ;
what he achieved*

CHAPTER ONE

Some definitions

In Part One, Chapter Two, we saw that the way a thing is done controls what the result will be. To make certain that the result you want actually happens, the right means must be used; to do a thing the right way makes certain that the purpose comes about. The scriptures make it clear that God (Father, Son and Spirit) intends to redeem men and women. The work of Christ is the means being used to do that. Since God always does things the right way, we must say that all who are actually redeemed are all he intended to redeem. Otherwise God would have failed to carry out his purpose.

Now it can be said that there were two purposes in the death of Christ, a primary one and a secondary one. The primary purpose of the death of Christ was to glorify God. In everything that he does, God intends, first, to display his own glory. All things exist primarily to bring glory to God for ever and ever (Ephesians 1:12; Philippians 2:11; Romans 11:36).

But the death of Christ also has a secondary purpose, that of saving men and women from their sins and bringing them to God. So I want to show you now that Christ's death has purchased, for everyone for whom he died, all that is necessary for them to enjoy such a salvation, without fail.

CHAPTER TWO

For whose good was Christ's death?

We need to be quite clear who actually benefits from Christ's death. There are three possibilities:

a. It could have been to benefit God the Father, or
b. It could have been to benefit himself, or
c. It could have been for our benefit

Remember, I am speaking here of the secondary purpose of the death of Christ; and in this sense, we can show that Christ's death was *not* in order to benefit God the Father.

Sometimes it is argued that Christ died in order to make it possible for God to forgive sinners, as though God would otherwise be unable to forgive us. This is to suggest that the secondary purpose of Christ's death was to benefit the Father. Such a view is both false and foolish for the following reasons:

1. It means that Christ died to set God the Father free from what stopped him doing what he wanted (i.e. forgiving sinners) rather than dying to free us from our sin. But scripture everywhere says plainly that Christ died *to set us free from sin.*
2. It means that no-one might actually be saved from sin. If Christ merely obtained the Father's freedom to forgive sinners, then the Father may – or may not – use that freedom! So Christ's death may still not actually obtain salvation for us. But scripture says plainly that Christ did come to *save the lost.*

Next, we can certainly show that Christ's death was not in order to benefit himself.

1. Since Christ is God, he already has all the glory and power he could have. So, at the close of his earthly life, he asks no other glory than he had before (John 17:5). He had no need to die to get any new benefits for himself.
2. Sometimes it is suggested that by his death Christ earned the right to be the judge of all. But if the aim of his death was to obtain the power to condemn some, then he cannot have died to save them! So even if we accept this suggestion, we cannot use it to prove that Christ died to save all men.

So we conclude that the death of Christ must have the purpose of benefiting *us*. It was not so that the Father might save us, if he would. It was not to obtain some new benefit for Christ himself. It must, therefore, be that Christ's death was actually to obtain all the good things that were promised by agreement with his Father, to benefit all those for whom he died. So he died only for those who actually receive those benefits. And it is to examine what the scripture says about those good things that we now pass.

CHAPTER THREE

What was the purpose of the death of Christ?

We have already said briefly what the scriptures teach about why Christ died (Part One, Chapter One). Now that we have explored the whole subject generally, we must examine in more detail those scriptures which

17

speak of what was to be achieved by Christ's death. I shall do this by examining three groups of Bible verses.

First, there are those scripture verses which show what God intended to do by the death of Christ. I have chosen eight verses for us to look at, though many more could be used.

1. Luke 19:10. "For the Son of Man has come to seek and to save that which was lost."
   Therefore it is clear that God intended actually to save lost sinners by Christ's death.
2. Matthew 1:21. "... you shall call his name Jesus, for it is he who will save his people from their sins".
   So whatever was necessary actually to save sinners was to be done by Jesus Christ.
3. I Timothy 1:15. "Christ Jesus came into the world to save sinners."
   This does not allow us to suppose that Christ came merely to make salvation for sinners possible; it insists that he came actually to save them.
4. Hebrews 2:14, 15. "... that he might render powerless him who had the power of death, that is, the devil; and might deliver those ... who were subject to slavery ...".
   What could be clearer than this? Christ came actually to deliver sinners.
5. Ephesians 5:25–27. "He gave himself for the church that he might sanctify her ... that he might present the church in all her glory ..."
   I do not think it is possible to say it more clearly than the Holy Spirit has done in this passage; Christ died to purify, sanctify and glorify the church.
6. John 17:19. "... I sanctify myself, that they themselves also may be sanctified".

18

Surely we must hear the Saviour himself declaring the purpose of his death? He died in order that some (not the whole world, since he did not pray for that – verse 9) should be truly sanctified (or made holy).

7. Galatians 1:4. "... who gave himself for our sins, that he might deliver us ...".

    Here again, it states the purpose of Christ's death as being actually to deliver us.

8. II Corinthians 5:21. "He made him who knew no sin to be sin on our behalf, that in him we might become the righteousness of God."

    So we learn that Christ came that sinners might become righteous.

From all these verses, it is clear that the death of Christ was intended to save, deliver, sanctify and make righteous those for whom he died. I ask, Are all men so saved, delivered, sanctified and made righteous? Or has Christ failed to fulfil his purpose? Judge for yourself, then, whether Christ died for all men, or only for those who are actually saved and made righteous!

Secondly, there are those scripture verses which speak not only of what was intended by Christ's death, but of what was actually obtained by it. Here I select six passages:

1. Hebrews 9:12, 14. "By his own blood, he ... obtained eternal redemption ... and ... cleanses your conscience from dead works."

    Here are mentioned two immediate results of the death of Christ – eternal redemption and cleansed consciences. Whoever has these is one for whom Christ died.

2. Hebrews 1:3. "When he had made purification of

sins, he sat down at the right hand of the Majesty on high."

So there is a spiritual cleansing obtained for those for whom Christ died.

3. I Peter 2:24. "He himself bore our sins."

   There you have a statement of what Christ did – he carried away our sins on the cross.

4. Colossians 1:21, 22. "He has now reconciled you ..."

   So an actual state of peace has been obtained between those for whom he died and God the Father.

5. Revelation 5:9, 10. "You were slain and have purchased us to God by your blood, out of every ... nation. And you have made us a kingdom of priests."

   Clearly this is not true of all men, but it does describe what is true of all for whom Christ died.

6. John 10:28. "I give eternal life to them ..."

   Christ himself explains that life is given to "his sheep" (verse 27). The spiritual life believers enjoy is obtained for them by the death of Christ.

From these six verses (and many more could be used), we can say the following: If the death of Christ actually obtains redemption, cleansing, purification, bearing away of sins, reconciliation, eternal life and citizenship in a kingdom, then he must have died only for those who do get those things. It is not true that all men have those things, as is very clear! The salvation of all men therefore cannot have been the purpose of the death of Christ.

Thirdly, there is also a group of scripture verses which describe those for whom Christ died. They are often described as "many" – e.g. Isaiah 53:11; Mark 10:45;

20

Hebrews 2:10. But these *many* are elsewhere described as:

the sheep of Christ	John 10:15
the children of God	John 11:52
the children God gave him	John 17:11; Hebrews 2:13
his elect	Romans 8:33
the people he foreknew	Romans 11:2
his church	Acts 20:28
those whose sins he took	Hebrews 9:28

Such descriptions are certainly not true of all men. So you see the purpose of the death of Christ, as it is set out in the scriptures, cannot have been the salvation of every man.

CHAPTER FOUR

Does the death of Christ make salvation a possibility, or a certainty?

Some have suggested that the death of Christ obtained redemption enough for all men, if only they would believe. That benefit, however, is only given to a few, because only a few believe. Christ, they say, obtained a salvation which is enough for everyone, but which actually saves only some.

Certainly, to pay a price for the redemption of a slave is not the same as actually setting the slave free. Obtaining salvation and giving salvation are not exactly the same. But there are several things that must now be understood as well:

1. Christ's obtaining our redemption, and then giving it to us may be two different acts; but it cannot be argued that therefore they must relate to two different groups of people. Christ did not have two purposes in his death!

2. God's will, that Christ should obtain salvation for sinners, did not depend on the condition that sinners believe. God's will was absolute that salvation should be obtained and given.

3. Our receiving of salvation is on condition of our faith. Yet that faith itself is given to us by God without conditions, as I hope to show later.

4. Those for whom Christ obtained benefits by his death must actually receive them. This is because:

    a. If Christ only obtained the benefits and could not give them, then his death might not save anyone!

    b. Did God appoint a Saviour without deciding who should be saved? Could he appoint a means without being sure of the end? That would be contrary to scripture teaching!

    c. If a thing is obtained for me, surely it must be mine by right, and whatever is mine by right must be mine in fact. So the salvation Christ obtained must belong to those for whom he obtained it. If it is said: "Yes, but it is theirs *on condition they believe*", I reply again, "But faith is also given by God".

    d. Scripture always joins together those for whom Christ obtained redemption, and those to whom he applies it.

i.   Isaiah 53:5.   Christ heals those for whom he was wounded.
ii. Isaiah 53:11.   Christ justifies those whose sins he bore.
iii. Romans 4:25.   Christ justifies those for whom he was delivered up.
iv. Romans 8:32–34.   God gives all things to those for whom Christ died.

> Those for whom Christ died cannot now be condemned.
>
> Christ now prays for those for whom he died.

From all these arguments it is firmly established that all those for whom Christ obtained redemption are certainly given it. Salvation was not made possible for all men by Christ's death; it was made actual for all *to whom it is given*.

Now let me make four statements which truly state this matter. On all these points I shall say more, later in the book.

1.   God sent Christ to die because of his eternal love to his elect.
2.   The value of Christ's death is beyond measurement, enough for everything intended to be done by it.
3.   The purpose of the Father was to bring from all nations many sons to glory, namely, his elect with whom he decided to make a new covenant.
4.   Everything purchased by the death of Christ for those people in due time certainly becomes theirs. Because he obtained it for them, Christ has reason to ask that this shall be so.

If we hold the view that Christ's death makes possible the salvation of all, but actually saves only those who believe, then we are really saying:

1. God ought to save all men. This we deny. God need only do what he freely chooses to do.
2. God cannot do what he wants, unless men fulfil certain conditions. This we deny. It takes away from the glory of God.
3. God's love is displayed better by his loving all men equally than by his loving only some men. This we deny, and will argue more fully in Part Four, Chapters Two and Four.
4. God sent his Son to die because he loved all men equally. This we deny, as unscriptural. Many scripture passages describe people who are clearly not the objects of the love that sent Christ to die. E.g. Proverbs 16:4; Acts 1:25; Romans 9:11–13; I Thessalonians 5:9; II Peter 2:12; Jude 4.
5. We are also saying that faith, which is the condition of receiving salvation, is not obtained for us by Christ's death. Scripture teaches that this faith *is* one of the benefits obtained for us by Christ.
6. We are saying that in his death, Christ was the substitute for all mankind. This we deny. For if Christ was the substitute for all, then all are saved.
7. We are saying that Christ died for those whom the Father knew would not be saved, since the Father foreknew all things. I do not see what is gained by such an argument!

CHAPTER FIVE

*Reasons why all for whom Christ died must actually
be saved*

I shall give one more chapter to show the error of the
strong opinion that the death of Christ was enough for
everyone's salvation, but actually saves some only.
("Sufficient for all, efficient for some"). Obtaining, and
giving, redemption are distinct, but they may not be
separated.

I argue that if anything is truly obtained for someone,
then it cannot be uncertain whether it is his. He will not
say, "It might be mine". So, whatever Christ obtained by
his death must belong to those for whom he obtained it.

It would be against common reason to suggest *God*
intended that Christ should die for someone – and yet
that person not receive the benefit.

It would be unreasonable that a ransom should be
paid for the redemption of slaves, and yet those slaves not
be set free! And we know that the death of Christ was a
ransom – Matthew 20:28.

Now some have argued that, while it is true that what
is obtained for someone is his by right, yet it might be
obtained for him *on certain conditions*. And, they say, the
condition on which we may receive the benefits Christ
obtained is that we do not resist the redemption offered,
or that we yield to the gospel invitation, or, simply, that
we have faith. Against this argument, I make the
following points:

1. If God's purpose to redeem anyone is made sin-
    cerely, and if Christ died to save everyone on certain
    conditions, then all and everyone must be made to

know these conditions. The purpose to save cannot be sincere if any are left uninformed of the conditions. What of those who never hear?

2. The required conditions to obtain the benefit of Christ's death must either be within our power to perform, or not. If they are, then all men have the power to believe; which is false. If not, then the Lord must grant that power, or not. If he does, why are not all saved? If he does not grant it, he cannot ask it as a condition, or he would be insincere in asking of us what only he can give us. It is as if one should promise a blind man £1,000, on condition that he can see it.

3. Faith – the condition of our enjoying salvation – is either obtained for us by Christ's death, or it is not. If it is, then all men have it; for, they say, Christ died for all. If it is not obtained for us by Christ, then the most vital part of our being saved does not depend on Christ at all! This takes away from the glory of Christ. And it is also contrary to the scripture teaching that faith is God's gift – Philippians 1:29; Ephesians 2:8.

4. To assert that Christ died for all, but that only those who fulfil certain conditions can be saved, is to make him only half a mediator. He has obtained salvation for all, they say. But what use is that, if he has not also fulfilled the conditions, say I!

So let me sum up. What Christ has obtained cannot be separated from those for whom he obtained it. Christ died, not that men should be saved if they would only believe; but he died for all God's elect, that they should believe. It is nowhere said in scripture, nor can it reasonably be affirmed, that Christ died for us if we believe.

26

That would be to make our believing the cause of what otherwise was not true – our act would make his death be for us! But Christ died for us that we might believe.

And now, having fully examined our subject, in Parts One and Two, we can proceed to study some proofs which establish the truth of what I maintain. As we do so, I want you to keep in your minds these fundamental points that we have made so far.

PART THREE

*Sixteen arguments which show that Christ did not ·
die for the salvation of all men*

Chapter

CHAPTER ONE

Two arguments based on the nature of the new covenant

Argument 1 In Matthew 26:28 the Lord Jesus Christ speaks of "my blood of the new testament". This new "testament", or "covenant" is the new agreement, or contract, God has made to save men. The blood of Christ, shed by his death, is the cost of that agreement, and that relates only to those to whom the agreement applies.

This new agreement is different from the old agreement that God made with men. By the old agreement (or covenant), God promised to save all who kept his laws: "The man who does these things will live by them" (Romans 10:5; Leviticus 18:5). But because men are sinners, they cannot keep God's laws. So the old agreement is made useless.

In the new agreement, God promises to put his laws in our minds and write them in our hearts (Hebrews 8:10). It is clear, then, that this agreement can only relate to those in whose hearts and minds God actually does this. Since God obviously does not do this for all men, all men cannot be included in the agreement by which Christ died.

Some have suggested that God would write his law in our minds if only we believed. But faith is the same thing as having God's law written in our hearts! So to talk as some do is to say: "If his law is in our hearts (i.e. as it is, in every believer), God promises he will write his law in our hearts" – which is nonsense!

The nature of the new covenant makes it clear that Christ's death was not for all men.

Argument 2 The gospel – in other words, the news about the new covenant – has been in the world through all the years since Christ. Yet whole nations have lived without any knowledge of it. If it was intended that the death of Christ should save all men, on condition that they believe, then the gospel ought to have been made known to all men.

If God has not arranged for all men to hear the gospel, then either it must be possible for men to be saved without faith and knowledge of the gospel; or, the purpose to save all men has failed, since all men have not heard. The former cannot be true, for faith is a part of salvation (see Part Two, Chapter Five). The latter cannot be true, either; would it be the nature of the wisdom of God to send Christ to die that all men might be saved, and yet never make sure all men heard of it? Is the goodness of God shown in such behaviour?

It is as if a doctor should say that he has a medicine that would cure everyone's diseases, yet deliberately hides that knowledge from many people. Can you really argue, in that case, that the doctor genuinely intended to cure everyone's diseases?

There are a number of scriptures which make it clear that millions never hear a word about Christ. And we can give no other reason for that than the reason Jesus himself gave: "Even so, Father, for so it seemed good in your sight" (Matthew 11:26). Such scriptures as Psalm 147:19, 20; Acts 14:16; Acts 16:6, 7, confirm the facts of our common experience that the Lord does not make any arrangement to ensure that all hear the gospel. We must conclude that it is not God's purpose to save all men.

CHAPTER TWO

Three arguments based on Bible descriptions of salvation

Argument 3 The scriptures describe what Jesus Christ obtained by his death as "eternal redemption". (This is our deliverance from sin, death and hell, for ever.) Now if this blessing was purchased for all men, then either all men *automatically* have this eternal redemption; or, it is available for all men *on fulfilment of certain conditions*.

In our experience, it is plainly not true that all men *have* eternal redemption. So, is eternal redemption, then, available *on certain conditions*?

I ask, did Christ satisfy those conditions for us, or does the satisfying of these conditions become ours only if further conditions are satisfied by us? The first of these – that Christ does fulfil all the conditions that must be met for eternal redemption to be given – would mean that all men do have this redemption; which, as we have already seen, does not agree with our experience of men! We have to say, then, that if Christ does not fulfil the conditions for all men to have redemption, he must fulfil those conditions only for those who fulfil further conditions. Now we run in a circle, making those conditions that are met depend on other conditions being met! These arguments show how unreasonable it is to suppose Christ died to obtain eternal salvation for all men.

If it is still insisted that eternal redemption is available on the fulfilment of certain conditions, then surely *all* men should be told? But many have this knowledge withheld from them, as we have seen in Part Three, Chapter One.

And further, if obtaining eternal redemption depends

on men fulfilling conditions, then either they have, or have not the power to do so. If they are able themselves to fulfil the necessary conditions, then we must say that all men can, of their own ability, believe the gospel. But this is quite contrary to scripture, which shows men dead in sin and therefore not able to fulfil any conditions.

If it is agreed that men do not themselves have the ability to fulfil the conditions for obtaining eternal redemption, then either God plans to give them this ability, or he does not. If he *does* so plan, why doesn't he do it? Then all men would be saved.

If, however, God does *not* intend to give all men the ability to believe, and yet Christ died that all men should have eternal redemption, then we have God requiring men to exercise abilities which he refuses to give them. Surely this is madness? It is as if God promises to give a dead man power to make himself alive, but at the same time has no intention of giving the man that promised power!

Argument 4 The Bible describes carefully those for whom Christ died. We are told that the human race can be divided into two groups, and that Christ died for only one of those groups.

Scriptures which show God dividing men into two groups are:

> Matthew 25:12 and 32
> John 10:14 and 26
> John 17:9
> Romans 9:11–23
> I Thessalonians 5:9

We learn that there are those whom God loves, and those

whom he hates; those whom he knows, and those whom he does not know.

Other scriptures make clear that Christ died for only one of these two groups. He died, we are told, for:

his people	Matthew 1:21
his sheep	John 10:11 and 14
his church	Acts 20:28
his elect	Romans 8:32–34
his children	Hebrews 2:13

Surely we must conclude from all this that Christ did not die for those who are not his people, or his sheep, or his church? He cannot therefore have died for all men.

Argument 5 We ought not to describe salvation in any way different from the way in which the Bible describes it. And the Bible nowhere says that Christ died "for all men", or for each and every man. It *is* said that Christ gave his life "a ransom for all"; however, it cannot be shown that this means more than "all his sheep" or "all his elect". If you look carefully at any verse which uses the word "all", and examine it in its context, you will soon be persuaded that nowhere does scripture say that Christ died for each and every man.

(In Part Four, Chapters Three and Four, we shall consider in detail many Bible verses in which the words "world" and "all" are used, in connection with the death of Christ.)

CHAPTER THREE

Two arguments based on the nature of Christ's work

Argument 6   There are many Bible verses which speak of the Lord Jesus Christ as making himself responsible for others when he died; for example:

He died *for us*	Romans 5:8
He was made a curse *for us*	Galatians 3:13
He was made sin *for us*	II Corinthians 5:21

Such expressions make it clear that Christ was doing something as a substitute for others.

Now if he died instead of others, it must follow that all those whose place he took must now be free from the anger and judgment of God. (God cannot justly punish both Christ *and* those whose substitute he was!) Yet it is clear that all men are not free from God's wrath (see John 3:36). Therefore Christ cannot have been the substitute for all men.

If it is still insisted that Christ did die as a substitute for all men, then we must conclude that his death was not a good enough sacrifice, for all men are not saved from sin and judgment!

Indeed, if Christ did die instead of all men, then either he offered himself a sacrifice for all their sins (in which case all men *are* saved), or it was a sacrifice for some of their sins only (in which case no-one is saved, for some sins remain). Neither of these statements can be true, as we have seen already in this book, (Part One, Chapter Three). It must be clear that there is no way we can say that Christ died for all men.

Argument 7   The scriptures describe the nature of the

work that Jesus Christ has done, as the work of a mediator and of a priest: "He is the mediator of a new covenant" (Hebrews 9:15). He acts as a mediator by being the priest of those whom he brings to God. That Jesus Christ is not the priest of everyone is obvious from experience, as well as from scripture; we have already discussed this in Part Two, Chapter Two.

CHAPTER FOUR

Three arguments based on the nature of holiness and faith

Argument 8   If the death of Christ is the means by which those for whom he died are cleansed from sin and made holy, then he must have died only for those who actually become so. It is obvious that all men are not made holy. Christ therefore did not die for all men.

Perhaps I should prove that the death of Christ is indeed the means of obtaining cleansing and holiness. I do this in two ways:

First, the Old Testament pattern of worship was designed to teach truths about the death of Christ. The blood of the Old Testament sacrifices did make it possible for those for whom it was shed, to come as acceptable worshippers to God. So how much more must the blood of Christ actually cleanse from sin those for whom he died? (Hebrews 9:13, 14).

Second, there are scripture verses that plainly state that the death of Christ does the very things it was intended to do; the body of sin is destroyed, that we should serve

37

sin no more (Romans 6:6); we have redemption through his blood (Colossians 1:14); he gave himself to redeem us, and to purify us (Titus 2:14). These verses, and many more, all insist that holiness is the certain result in the lives of all for whom Christ died. Since all men are not holy, Christ did not die for all men.

Some suggest – vainly! – that Christ's death is not the only cause of this holiness. They say that it only becomes actual or real when the Holy Spirit brings it, or when it is received by faith. But the work of the Holy Spirit, and the gift of faith, are also the result or fruit of Christ's death! So this suggestion does not alter the fact that actual holiness is the certain result only in the lives of those for whom Christ died. The fact that the judge gives permission and the gaoler unlocks the prison door, is not the cause of the debtor being set free; the cause is that someone paid his debts for him.

Argument 9   Faith is essential to salvation. This is clear from scripture (Hebrews 11:6) and most people accept the fact. But, as we have already seen, all that is necessary for salvation has been obtained for us by Christ.

Now if this essential faith is obtained for all men by Christ, it is ours either with, or without, some conditions. If it is without conditions, then all men have it. But that is contrary to experience, and to scripture (II Thessalonians 3:2). If faith is given only on some condition, then I ask: On what condition?

Some say, Faith is given on condition that we do not resist God's grace. Yet, not to resist really means to obey. To obey means to believe. So what these friends are really saying is, "Faith is granted to those who believe" (i.e. those who have faith!) This is plainly absurd.

On the other hand, some argue that faith is *not* obtained for us by Christ's death. Is faith then an act of our own wills? But that is quite contrary to what many Bible verses teach, and ignores the fact that unbelievers are dead in sin, unable to perform any spiritual act, (I Corinthians 2:14). So I shall return to the position that faith is obtained by Christ.

Faith is an essential part of holiness. In Argument 8, I showed that holiness is obtained for us by the death of Christ. Therefore he also obtained faith for us. To deny this is to say that he obtained only a partial holiness, i.e. lacking faith. No-one seriously suggests this.

Moreover, God chose his people, we are told, in order that they might be holy; God "has chosen us ... that we should be holy" (Ephesians 1:4). Again, faith is an essential part of holiness. In choosing his people to be holy, God must choose that they shall have faith.

It was part of the agreement between God the Father and God the Son that all for whom Christ died shall have the blessings the Father intends to give them. Faith is one of the blessings the Father gives (Hebrews 8:10, 11).

Scriptures clearly state that faith is obtained for us by Jesus Christ, who is "the author and finisher of our faith" (Hebrews 12:2). Statements such as this and the statements of the previous three paragraphs you have just read, all confirm that the death of Christ obtains faith for his people. Since all men do not have it, Christ cannot have died for all men.

Argument 10 The people of Israel were, in many ways, a kind of illustration of the New Testament church of God (I Corinthians 10:11). Their priests and sacrifices were examples of what Jesus Christ was coming to do for the church of God. Their city,

39

Jerusalem, is used as a picture of the believer's heaven (Hebrews 12:22). A true Israelite is a believer (John 1:47) and a true believer is an Israelite (Galatians 3:29). So I argue this way:

If the nation of the Jews was chosen by God, *out of all the nations in the world*, to illustrate his dealings with the church, then it follows that the death of Christ was only for the church and not for all the world. The way God treated his chosen people in the Old Testament is an illustration of how the salvation Christ obtained is not for all men, but is for his chosen people alone.

CHAPTER FIVE

An argument based on the meaning of the word "Redemption"

Argument 11   The way in which the Bible describes a doctrine must help us to understand the doctrine. One Bible word used to describe the salvation Christ obtained, is the word *redemption*; e.g. "We have redemption through his blood" (Colossians 1:14). That word means "to free a person from captivity by paying a price". The person is not redeemed unless he is *freed*. So the very word teaches us that Christ cannot have obtained redemption for any who are not freed. A universal redemption (so-called!) which finally leaves any still in captivity is a contradiction in terms.

The blood of Christ is actually called a price, and a ransom, in some Bible verses (e.g. Matthew 20:28). Now the purpose of a ransom is to obtain the deliverance of those for whom the price if paid. It is unthinkable that a ransom be paid and the person still remain a prisoner. So how can it be argued that Christ died for all men, when all men are not saved? Only those who are actually freed from sin can be those for whom Christ died. "Redemption" cannot be "universal" any more than "Roman" can be "catholic"! Redemption must be particular, since only some are redeemed.

CHAPTER SIX

An argument based on the meaning of the word "Reconciliation"

Argument 12 Another word the Bible uses to describe what Christ obtained by his death is the word *reconciliation*; "enemies ... he reconciled ..." (Colossians 1:21). Reconciliation is restoring friendship between two parties formerly enemies. In the salvation of which the Bible speaks, God is reconciled to us, and we are reconciled to God. Both these things must be true; the reconciling of the one party and of the other *are* two separate acts, but both are required to make a complete reconciliation. It is foolish to suggest that God is, through Christ's death, now reconciled to all men, but that only some men are reconciled to him. I hope no-one does suggest that God and all men are reconciled in this way. That would be a reconciliation hopping on one leg! There is no proper reconciliation unless both parties are reconciled to each other.

The effect of Christ's death was to reconcile both God

to men *and* men to God; "we were reconciled to God through the death of his son" (Romans 5:10) and "our Lord Jesus Christ, through whom we have now received the reconciliation" (Romans 5:11). So also both reconciliations are mentioned in II Corinthians 5:19, 20 – "God ... reconciling ... to himself", and "you ... be reconciled to God".

Now how this double reconciliation can be "reconciled" with the notion of Christ's death being for all men, I cannot see! For if all men are, by Christ's death, so doubly reconciled, how does it happen that God's wrath is upon any? (John 3:36). Surely, Christ can only have died for those who are actually reconciled?

CHAPTER SEVEN

An argument based on the meaning of the word "Satisfaction"

Argument 13   It is true that the word *satisfaction* is not used in the English Bible, with reference to the death of Christ. But the thing that the word means, i.e. "a full payment of what is due to a creditor by a debtor" is a thought often used in the New Testament, when it speaks of the death of Christ.

In our case, men are debtors to God, for they fail to keep his commandments. The satisfaction required to pay for our sin is death – "the wages of sin is death" (Romans 6:23). God's laws are our accusers, expressing God's justice and truth. We stand convicted as lawbreakers, deserving therefore to die. Salvation is only

42

possible if Christ shall pay our debt, and so satisfy the justice of God. His death is called "an offering" (Ephesians 5:2) and a "propitiation" (I John 2:2). The word *offering* means a sacrifice of expiation, or a sacrifice to make amends for sin. *Propitiation* means an offering to satisfy offended justice. So, we may rightly use the word *satisfaction* to cover the whole Bible teaching as to the meaning of Christ's death.

Now if Christ has indeed by his death made satisfaction for any, then God must now be fully satisfied with them. God cannot justly require a second payment of any sort. How then can it be that Christ died for all men, and yet many live and die as sinners under the condemnation of God's law? Let them that can, reconcile these things! I say that only those who are actually freed from debt in this life can be the ones for whom Christ made satisfaction.

CHAPTER EIGHT

Two arguments based on the value of the death of Christ

Argument 14   The New Testament does often speak of the worth or value of the death of Christ, with which he was able to purchase and obtain certain things. E.g. eternal redemption is said to be "obtained by his blood" (Hebrews 9:12); the church of God is said to be "bought with his own blood" (Acts 20:28); and Christians are called "a purchased people" (I Peter 2:9, English A.V. margin).

Christ then, by his death, purchased, for all for whom he died, all those things which the Bible says were the effects of his death. The value of his death purchased deliverance from the power of sin and God's wrath, from death and the power of the devil, from the curse of the law and the guilt of sin. The value of his death obtained reconciliation with God, peace, and eternal redemption. These things are now God's free gifts, because Christ purchased them. If Christ died for all men, then why do not all men have these things? Is the value of his death not enough? Is God unjust, not to give us what Christ bought for us? It must be immediately obvious that Christ cannot have died to purchase these things for all men, but only for those who actually enjoy them.

Argument 15 Phrases often used of the death of Christ are such as: dying *for* us, bearing *our* sins, being our *surety*. The plain meaning of such phrases is that Christ, in his death, was a substitute for others, that they might go free.

If, in his death, Christ was a substitute for others, how can they themselves also die still bearing their own sins? Christ could not have been a substitute for them. From which it is clear that he cannot have died for all men.

Indeed, to say Christ died for all men is the quickest way to prove he died for no-one. For if he died instead of all, and yet all are not saved, then he failed in his purpose.

CHAPTER NINE

A general argument from particular verses of scripture

Argument 16   There are a great number of Bible verses I could use, to argue that Christ did not die for the sins of all men. I will select just nine, and with them close our arguments in this part.

1. Genesis 3:15   This is the first Bible verse in which God indicates there is a difference between the people of God and their enemies. By "the seed of the woman" is meant Jesus Christ and then also all believers in Christ. (This is clear from the fact that what is prophesied of the woman's seed is fulfilled in Christ and in his people.) By "the seed of the serpent" is meant all unbelieving men of the world (compare John 8:44). Since God promised only hatred between the seed of the serpent and the seed of the woman, it is obvious that Christ the seed of the woman did not die for the seed of the serpent!

2. Matthew 7:23.   Christ here states that there are people whom he has never known. Yet, in another place (John 10:14-17) he says he does know all his own people. He must surely know all for whom he died? If there are some he does not know, he cannot have died for them.

3. Matthew 11:25-27.   From these words it is clear that there are some from whom God hides the gospel. If it is the Father's will that they shall not have the gospel revealed to them, Christ cannot have died for them. And we should note that Christ here gives thanks to the Father for making this difference

45

between men – a difference which some men still refuse to believe!

4. John 10:11, 15, 16, 27, 28. From these verses it is quite clear that:

   i. All men are not Christ's sheep.

   ii. The difference between men will one day be obvious.

   iii. Christ's sheep are identified as "those who hear Christ's voice"; others do not hear it.

   iv. Some who are not yet identified as sheep are already chosen and will become known ("other sheep").

   v. Christ died, not for all, but specifically for his sheep.

   vi. Those for whom Christ died are those given to him by his Father. He cannot, then, have died for those not so given to him.

5. Romans 8:32–34. From these verses it is plain that the death of Christ belongs only to God's elect people, and also that Christ's intercesssion is only for the same people.

6. Ephesians 1:7. From this verse we must say that if Christ's blood was shed for all, then all must have this redemption and forgiveness. But most certainly all do not have them.

7. II Corinthians 5:21. So, in his death, Christ was made sin for all those who are made the righteousness of God in him. If he was sin for all, why are not all made righteousness?

8. John 17:9. Christ's intercession is not for all men, and therefore neither was his death. (See Part Two, Chapters Four and Five.)

9. Ephesians 5:25. Christ loves the church, and that is an example of how a man should love his wife.

But if Christ loved others as well as his church, so as to die for them, then men may surely love other women besides their wives!

I did think I could add other arguments – but, on looking over what I have already said, I am confident that what has been already argued is enough to satisfy any who will be satisfied with anything; those who are obstinate will not be satisfied if I do include more. So I end my arguments here.

PART FOUR

*Arguments for universal
redemption answered*

N.B. In this section, the arrangement of chapters is a little different from John Owen's, to make for slightly clearer presentation.

CHAPTER ONE

Answers to four general reasons often given for a universal redemption

Reason 1 There are passages of scripture which speak of what Christ achieved by his death, in very general and indefinite terms. Therefore, it is argued, his death cannot have been for a particular or limited purpose.

For example, the scriptures speak of the infinite worth of the death of Christ. It is spoken of as the shedding of "God's own blood" (Acts 20:28). The death of Christ is said to be an offering "without blemish" which is offered through "the eternal Spirit" (Hebrews 9:14). The blood of Christ is described as "precious", more precious than silver or gold (I Peter 1:18). Now, if the death of the Son of God possesses such obvious and infinite worth, must it not be sufficient for all men?

We do not deny that Christ's death was of sufficient worth to redeem all men. Our point is, the scriptures make it clear that Christ's death was not intended to be a ransom for every man. This argument is worked out more fully in Chapters Two, Three, Four, Five and Six. Some may object: If Christ did not die for all, then it is useless to preach to all, which we are commanded to do (Matthew 28:19). To this I reply:

a. There are some to be saved from every nation, which cannot be done unless the gospel is preached to all nations.

b. Since there are now no special privileges for the one nation of the Jews, the gospel must be preached to all without distinction.

c. The call to men to believe, is not a call, in the first

place, to believe that Christ died for them in particular, but a call to believe that there is no other than
Jesus through whom salvation is preached.

d. Preachers can never know who, in their congre-
gations, are God's elect. They must therefore call on
all to believe, and promise that as many as do will
be saved, for there is enough in the death of Christ to
save everyone who believes.

These points should be enough to make it clear that the
gospel is to be preached to all, though all will not be
saved.

(At this point, John Owen has a long section on the use of
the terms "world" and "all men", which we have moved
to Chapters Two and Six respectively.)

Reason 2   The scriptures sometimes seem to suggest
that some for whom Christ died are not actually saved.
From this it is suggested that Christ must have died for
all, but only some succeed in fulfilling the right conditions.

We need to understand that the scriptures often
describe people by their outward appearance, not by their
true inward state. For example, Jerusalem is called "the
holy city" (Matthew 27:53). We are not therefore to
understand that Jerusalem was actually holy.

Similarly, the scriptures often describe people as
"holy" or "saints" or even as "elect" because they were
outwardly connected with the communities of believers.
Paul said, of the Philippian believers: "it is right for me
to think this way of you" (Philippians 1:7). We cannot
conclude from this that all to whom Paul wrote were
actually believers. Paul was judging them from the best
of his knowledge of them. So if some fell away, we cannot

say that God intended to save all but only some held on. Whoever falls away, never was a true believer, despite his outward appearance of being one. (This argument is worked out more fully in Chapter Seven.)

Reason 3 The scriptures sometimes suggest that salvation is offered generally to all, if only they will believe. From this it is concluded that Christ must have died for all.

It is true that faith and salvation are always linked, in the scriptures. He who believes shall be saved. But this means no more than that all believers shall certainly be saved. It cannot mean that God intends to save all, if they will believe, because:

a. God does not, in fact, offer eternal life to all men. A greater part of mankind has never heard the gospel.
b. God's general commands do not tell us what his particular intentions may be. In general, it is his command that men obey him. But in the particular case of Pharaoh, for example, God's intentions were different from his commands, for he hardened Pharaoh's heart (Exodus 4:21), while commanding him to obey.
c. The promise of the gospel does teach an unbreakable connection between faith and salvation. But this cannot mean that God intends all to repent and believe, for what then is the purpose of divine election? If he intended to save all, why elect only some? And anyway, if he intended to save all, why has he failed to carry out his intention? (It is of no use to suggest he failed because men would not believe; he must have known beforehand that they

53

would not believe; why, then, intend what he knew
he could not fulfil?)

Also, the fact that believers and unbelievers live mixed
together, and the preacher cannot certainly tell who are,
and who are not, the elect of God, means that he must
preach in general terms to all. This does not mean that
the gospel promise is made generally to all, but merely
that it is declared generally to all. Since Christ is only
received by faith, and since faith is God's gift to whom he
pleases, it is clear he cannot intend the salvation of any to
whom he does not give faith.

Reason 4   If Christ did not die for all men, then surely
the scripture exhortations that all should believe, are
without value?

It needs to be understood that the faith of which
the scriptures speak has various stages of growth, and a
logical order of use. We are not to think that scripture
exhortations to believe require everyone to believe that
Christ died for him in particular. There are other things
to be believed, which all men can receive. No-one is
commanded to believe anything he does not have sufficient evidence for. For example:

a.   The first thing that men are to believe is that they
     cannot save themselves, because they are sinners.
     Every man has the evidence for this in himself, as
     Paul shows in Romans, Chapters 1, 2 and 3. How
     many will not even come as far as to believe this,
     though they have plenty of evidence for it!

b.   The gospel calls sinners to believe that God has
     provided a way of salvation by Jesus Christ.
     Millions have heard of this, but refuse to accept it,
     despite plenty of evidence for it!

54

c.   The gospel calls sinners to believe that there is no other Saviour of men than Jesus Christ. This was the very thing the Jews refused to believe, calling Christ an enemy of God instead!

These general calls are not made because Christ died for all, but because these truths are evident to all. And only after these acts of faith are done, is anyone called to believe that Jesus died for him in particular. It has been noted by some that the Apostles' Creed (that ancient summary of Christian Religion) puts last of the things to be believed, "the forgiveness of sins and the life eternal"; that is to say, before we can come so far, there are other things which must be believed; and for which there is plenty of evidence. We return to this argument again in Chapter Eight.

CHAPTER TWO

Preliminary explanation of those verses using the word "world"

In one sense I am reluctant to mention any passage of scripture which has been used to support the idea that Christ died for all men. This is not because such verses are hard for me to explain, but because I am unwilling even to mention such an untruth. But I suppose most of these verses will already have been brought to the notice of my readers by those who hold to that error. So I must now give you the answers with which to reply to them.

Do not be carried away by the mere sound of words.

55

Always remember what is the general trend of Bible teaching, and never interpret a verse contrary to the general trend of the whole scripture. For example, we can show that the word "world" must mean what the surrounding verses of any one place make it mean; there are five different usages of the word.

1.	The material universe, or habitable earth	Job 34:13
		Matthew 13:38
		Acts 17:24
		Ephesians 1:4
		and many other places
2.	The people of the world, as	
	All without exception	Romans 3:6
	All without difference	John 7:4
	Many men	Matthew 18:7
	Most men	Romans 1:8
	The Roman Empire	Luke 2:1
	Good men	John 6:33
	Bad men	John 14:17
		and many other places
3.	The world as a corrupt system	Galatians 6:14
		and many other places
4.	The human state	John 18:36
		and many other places
5.	Satan's kingdom	John 14:30
		and many other places

Some may object that a word must always have the same meaning wherever it occurs in scripture. I answer: That cannot be correct, for there are some places where scripture uses different meanings for the same word in the same sentence. In Matthew 8:22 "dead" means first, spiritually dead, and second, physically dead. In John

1:10 "world" means first, the habitable earth; second, the planet earth, and third, some men on the earth.

Also, if the word "world" is *sometimes* used to mean less than all men, then it cannot be argued that it must always mean all men. And there are several places where the word clearly means less than all men.

Luke 2:1 – "all the world". This clearly means the Roman Empire. It cannot meant everyone in the world.

John 1:10 – "the world knew him not". But some men did believe in him. "World" therefore cannot mean everyone.

John 8:26 – "I speak to the world". But only certain Jews heard him speak. "World" cannot mean everyone.

John 12:19 – "the world is gone after him". This can only mean most of the Jewish nation had gone after him. It cannot mean everyone.

I John 5:19 – "the whole world". But there are many true believers in the world who are obviously not in the power of the wicked one. "World" cannot mean everyone.

So the word "world" commonly means only some men in the world. I see no reason why the word should be made to mean anything else in those places where it is used in connection with salvation.

After these general observations, let us come to some scripture verses using the term "world", such as John 1:29; 3:16; 4:42; 6:51; II Corinthians 5:19 and I John 2:2. Using such verses, some argue:

1. The world contains all and every man.

2. Christ is said to die for the world.
3. Therefore, Christ died for all and every man.

This reasoning is at fault, because the word "world" is being used in two different senses. In the first statement, "world" means the planet earth. In the second statement, it is used to mean the people of the world. There is no common meaning between the two statements. So the conclusion must be false (unless you wish to prove that Christ died for the planet earth).

Some have tried to re-write the argument thus:

1. In some places in scripture, "world" means all and every man.
2. Christ is said to die for the world.
3. Therefore, Christ died for all and every man.

This argument is also at fault, because you cannot deduce a universal conclusion when the first statement only refers to the limited meaning of a word or phrase, as with "some places". Also, I must insist that in many places, the death of Christ is related only to "his sheep" or "his church".

So, again, the argument needs to be re-written, as:

1. In some places in scripture the world "world" means all and every man.
2. In some places in Scripture Christ is said to die for the whole world.
3. Therefore, Christ died for all and every man.

That this argument is ridiculous must be evident to anyone! It needs to be shown that the "some places" of statement 1 are the same as the "some places" in statement 2. Failing that, the argument proves nothing.

And, in any case, a universal conclusion cannot be drawn from a limited first statement, as we saw before.

So, in a preliminary way, I think I have exposed the errors of arguments based on the use of the word "world". I dare to say that weaker arguments were never produced in so weighty a cause by thinking men! But leaving aside arguments alone, let us come to the scriptures themselves.

CHAPTER THREE

A detailed study of John 3:16

This verse is often taken to teach that:

"loved"	— 1.	God has such a natural longing for the good of
"world"	= 2.	the whole human race of all ages and times, that
"gave"	= 3.	he gave his Son to die, not actually to save any, but
"whosoever"	= 4.	so that any who have the natural tendency to believe
"have"	= 5.	can thereby obtain eternal life.

In contrast to this, we understand the verse to teach that:

"loved"	= 1.	God had such a special, supreme, love that he willed
"world"	= 2.	that, of all races, his whole people should be saved

"gave"	= 3.	by appointing his Son to be an all-sufficient Saviour
"whosoever"	= 4.	making it certain that all believers whatsoever, and only they
"have"	= 5.	shall effectively have all the glorious things he intends for them.

There are three things to be carefully studied here. First, the love of God; second, the object of God's love, here called "the world"; third, the intention of God's love, that believers "should not perish".

1. It is important to understand that nothing which suggests that God is imperfect is to be said of him. His work is perfect. But if it be argued that he has a natural longing for the salvation of all, then the failure of all to be saved must mean that his longing is weak, and his happiness incomplete.

Also, scripture nowhere asserts that God is naturally inclined to the good of all. On the contrary, it is evident that God is able freely to have mercy on whom he will have mercy. His love is a free act of his will, not an emotion produced in him by our miserable state. (If it was misery that attracted God's natural longing to help, then he ought to be merciful to the devils and the damned!)

The love which is here described is a special and supreme act of God's will, directed particularly toward believers. The words "so" and "in order that" emphasise the unusual manner of this love, and the clear purpose of it to save believers from perishing. This love, then, cannot be a common affection toward all, some of whom do perish.

Other scripture verses also agree that this love of God is a supreme act, and is especially toward believers, as for example, Romans 5:8 or I John 4:9, 10. One would not speak of a natural inclination for the good of all in such emphatic ways as these.

It is clear that God wills the good of those whom he loves. Then it must follow that he loves only those who receive that good. The same love that caused him to give Christ, causes him to give all other needed things, too. "He who did not spare his own Son, but delivered him up for us all, how will he not also with him freely give us all things?" (Romans 8:32). So, this special love of God can therefore only be to those who actually have grace and glory given to them.

Now, Christian reader, you must judge; can the love of God, who thus gave his Son, be understood as a general goodwill in him toward all? Is it not rather his special love toward elect believers?

2.   We must examine what the object of this love of God is, here called "the world". Some say: This must mean all and every man. I have never been able to see how it could mean this. We have already shown with what different meanings the word "world" is used in scripture. And in John 3:16, the love mentioned at the beginning, and the purpose at the end, cannot possibly agree with the meaning of "all and every man" which is, by some, imposed on "the world" in the middle of the verse!

For our part, the word is understood to mean the elect of God scattered abroad in the world among all nations. No longer are the special benefits of God to be for the Jews alone. The sense is, "God so loved his elect throughout the world, that he gave his Son with this intention, that by him believers might be saved". There are several reasons to support this view.

The nature of God's love, as we have already examined it here, cannot possibly be thought of as extending to all and every man. The "world", in this verse, must be whatever world it is that actually receives eternal life. This is confirmed by the very next verse – John 3:17 – where, in the third occurrence of the term "world", it is said that God's purpose in sending Christ was "in order that the world should be saved". If "world" here is understood of any but elect believers, then God has failed in his purpose; we dare not allow that.

It is not unusual, in fact, for God's believing people to be called by such terms as "world", "all flesh", "all nations" and "all families of the earth". For example, in John 4:42, Christ is said to be the Saviour of the world. A Saviour of men not saved would be a contradiction in terms. So, those who are here called "the world" must be only those who are saved.

There are several reasons why believers are called "the world". It is to distinguish them from angels; to reject boastful Jews who thought themselves alone God's people; to teach the distinction between the old covenant made with one nation, and the new – when all parts of the world were to be made obedient to Christ; and to show the natural condition of believers as earthly, worldly creatures.

If it still be argued that "world" here does mean all and every man as the object of God's love, then why has not God revealed Jesus to everyone he so loved? Strange! that God should give his Son for them, and yet never tell them of his love – millions have never heard the gospel! How can he be said to love every man, if his providence means that this love is not known by every man?

Finally, "world" cannot mean all and every man unless you are ready to allow:

God's love toward many is in vain, because they perish.

Christ was given for millions who never knew of him.

Christ was given for millions who cannot believe in him.

God changes his love, to forsake those who perish (or else, he continues to love them in hell).

God fails to give all things to those for whom he gave Christ.

God does not know beforehand who will believe and be saved.

Such absurdities we cannot grant; "world" can only mean those persons scattered throughout the world who are the elect.

3.   The way in which the elect of God actually come to obtain the life that is in his Son is said to be by believing. It is "every believer that shall not perish".*

If it be argued that Christ died for all and every man, and yet now we learn that only believers shall be saved, what makes the difference between believers and unbelievers? They cannot make the difference themselves (see I Corinthians 4:7). Then God made them to differ. But if God made them to differ, how can he have given Christ for them all?

The verse declares God's intention that believers shall

* It does not help the cause of universal atonement to suggest that "whosoever" means "anyone", indefinitely.

1:   The form of the Greek words actually is "every believer".

2.   To argue for "anyone" is effectively to deny that God's love is equally to every man! If some – "the whosoever" can be especially favoured, then God cannot have loved all men equally. He must somehow have loved "the whosoevers" more than the rest!

63

be saved. Then it follows that God did not give his Son for unbelievers. How could he have given his Son for those to whom he did not give the grace to believe?

Now let the reader weigh-up all these things, and especially the first, the love of God, and seriously ask whether that can be a general affection to all, which can tolerate the perishing of many of these so loved? Or, is not this love better understood to be that unique, special love of the Father to his believing children, which makes their future secure? Then you will have an answer as to whether scripture teaches that Christ died as a general ransom – fruitless in respect of many for whom it must then have been paid – or as a particular redemption gloriously effectual for every believer. And remember, this verse John 3:16 is so often used to support the idea that Christ died for every man – though, as I have shown, it is completely inconsistent with such a notion!

CHAPTER FOUR

A detailed study of I John 2:1–2

This is another verse of scripture often used by those who would argue that Christ's death is for all and every man. It is said that the phrase "the whole world" must mean "all people in the world", and that the contrasting phrase "not for ours only" does deliberately include all and every man as those for whom Christ died, in addition to the believers.

I could answer this briefly, by saying that as, in other places, "the world" means "people living in the world", so "the whole world" means no more than "people living throughout the whole world", as the redeemed are said to be in Revelation 5:9. But since so much use is made of this verse in 1 John, I shall suggest a more detailed study, using four questions.

1.   To whom is John writing? While it is true that the scriptures are for the whole church, yet many parts of it were written to special people. Such scriptures must be understood in the light of that fact. So we note:

a.   That John was especially an apostle to Jews – Galatians 2:9.
b.   He writes to those who have previously heard God's Word (I John 2:7) and we know that God's Word was "to the Jew first".
c.   The contrast that John makes between "us" and "the world" makes it clear that he writes to those who, like himself, were Jews.
d.   John frequently cautions against false teachers – for example, I John 2:19. Since he writes of such teachers "going out from us", he is obviously writing to fellow Jews.

Remembering the Jewish national hatred of all Gentiles, and the Jewish opinion that their nation alone was God's people, what could be more natural than that John should emphasise that Jesus died, not for believing Jews alone, but for all believers throughout the whole world? We have another scripture expressing that same emphasis, in John 11:52. John is clearly concerned to prevent Jewish Christians falling into the old error of supposing they were the only Christians. John insists there are Gentile Christians, too, throughout the world. There is no doctrine here of Christ dying for all men.

65

2. Why was John writing? He wrote in order to give comfort to believers troubled by their sins, so that they need not despair. "If any man sin ..." From which we note:

a. Only believers would be comforted that Christ is their advocate.
b. Only believers can be comforted; unbelievers are under God's wrath.
c. John describes them as "little children ... whose sins are forgiven".

In other words, John's aim only applies to believers. How can it be a comfort to believers to be told that Christ died for all and every man, many of whom are not saved? The verse gives no comfort, unless it is understood to mean Christ is the Saviour of all believers anywhere in the world.

3. What is the meaning of "propitiation"? The Greek word here translated as "propitiation" is related to the word translated "mercy-seat" in Hebrews 9:5. This usage gives us an understanding of the meaning of the word. The "mercy-seat" was the solid slab of gold used to cover the Ark, in which were the tables of the Law (Exodus 25:17–22). The Law, which accused men of being sinners, was hidden by the mercy-seat. That was a picture of how Jesus Christ, by his death, has hidden God's Law so that it cannot accuse any who believe in him. Jesus is the believer's propitiation (mercy-seat). Can it really be said that all and everyone in the world is free from being condemned as a sinner? Can it really be argued that Christ is the propitiation of the whole world, in this sense?

4. What then is the meaning of "the WHOLE world"?

66

This phrase occurs several times in the New Testament and often does NOT mean each and every man. For example:

Luke 2:1.   But only the Roman Empire was thus taxed.

Romans 1:8.   But many parts of the world had not heard of the church in Rome at that time.

Colossians 1:6.   But many parts of the world had not then received the gospel.

Revelation 3:10.   The whole world is to suffer – but this does not mean everyone, for some are to be kept from it.

In these, and other places, the whole world means no more than many people, indefinitely.

Also, in a number of scriptures, phrases like "all flesh" mean no more than all kinds of people, as, for example:

Psalm 98:3;   Joel 2:28 (fulfilled in Acts 2:17)

Sometimes, indeed, the whole world means all EXCEPT Christian believers, as, for example:

I John 5:19;   Revelation 12:9

Clearly these examples show that it is not essential to understand the phrase "the whole world" in an "all-inclusive" way. The meaning need be no more than the context of the phrase sensibly allows.

I conclude that this passage of scripture refers to Christ's work for all believers, Jewish and Gentile alike. It says that he actually is their propitiation. No-one seriously argues that all men, everywhere, are actually saved by Christ. Nor is it any help to suggest that Christ is a sufficient propitiation for each and every man. Jacob would not have been comforted merely to hear that there was sufficient corn in Egypt. He would have starved had not the corn been made actually his. So Christ is only a comfort to those who are actually saved, throughout the whole world.

CHAPTER FIVE

Brief explanations of six passages of scripture

Among other scriptures sometimes used to suggest that Christ died for all men, are the following:

1.　John 1:9.　This verse is probably best translated as: "That was the true light, which, coming into the world, lights every man." (Compare also John 3:19 and 12:46.)

In other words, Christ coming into the world has had an enlightening effect on men; anyone, having any light of truth, has it from Christ. This is a weak place indeed on which to base any argument for universal redemption.

2.　John 1:29.　That Christ takes away the sin common to all the world in general is most certain. But that he takes sin away from and purges it out of all and every man, is not true either in this verse or in our experience!

3.　John 3:17.　This cannot be understood to mean that Christ died for all men, for:
　　a.　All men are not in fact saved.
　　b.　Many were already condemned when Christ came.

     c.   Christ was appointed for the fall of some (Luke 2:34).

     d.   The aim of Christ's coming cannot have been different from God's eternal purposes, which already involved the condemnation of some because of their sins. Did God send his Son to save such?

The world saved here according to his purpose is the world of all the people of God.

4.   John 4:42 and I John 4:14.   We understand Christ to be called the Saviour of the world in the sense:

     a.   That there is no other Saviour for any in the world, and

     b.   He alone saves all that are saved, all over the world.

Obviously he cannot be called the Saviour of the world because he has actually saved everyone – for he has not.

5.   John 6:51.   The fact that "the world" in this place does not mean all and every one should be as clear as daylight! The verse states that Christ was to give his life that others should have life. Can we really suppose that all men everywhere have his life? Do those damned already have his life? For we must say "yes" to both of those questions, if "world" means each and every man.

6.   II Corinthians 5:19.   Here again we must draw the meaning of the word "world" from its context. Those called "world" in verse 19 are called "us" in verse 18 and "we" in verse 21. The things spoken of in all these places are only true of believers. "World", here, means those whose trespasses are forgiven.

If "world" here is taken to mean every man in the world, then why are not all men reconciled to God? It is not said that God will reconcile all, on certain conditions, but that he has actually done so!

This is our defence, and answer, to those who twist these passages of scripture to support their idea that Christ died for all. The whole strength of their argument in these places rests on the one word "world", which is a most ambiguous word! Let the reader "prove all things, and hold fast to what is good".

CHAPTER SIX

Explanation of those verses using the words "all men" or "every man"

There are some general things that need to be said first, about the use of the word "all". It has two meanings in normal use. It can either mean "the entire number of", or, "those of every sort". I am prepared to say that not more than once in ten times does it mean "the entire number", in scripture! The most common usage is to mean "those of every sort". For example:

Luke 11:42.　The actual words here are "all herbs". But the translators have made it read "all manner of herbs", which we believe is correct.

John 12:32.　Obviously, the entire human race is not drawn to Christ. "All", in this place, can only mean men of all sorts.

Acts 2:17.　It is clear from experience that the Holy

Spirit is not poured out on the whole human race.
"All flesh" can only mean people of every sort – not
Jews only.

Acts 10:12.   Again, the actual words are "all beasts".
But the translators have correctly written "all manner of beasts".

From these examples (and we could use many others), we
draw three conclusions:

a.   The word "all" often means "some of every sort".
b.   The word "all" can mean "every one of a particular
     sort". In Romans 5:18 "all men" obviously means
     "all justified men", or, "all believers".
c.   When the Old Testament prophesies that "all
     nations" shall be converted, the New Testament
     shows that the elect of God from every nation is
     meant.

After these general observations, I come to several particular passages of scripture, which are often used by those
who wish to argue that Christ died for all the human
race.

1.   Perhaps the chief among these passages is
I Timothy 2:4–6. From these verses it is argued:

> If God will have all men saved, then Christ must
> die for all men. But it is here said that God will
> have all men to be saved. Therefore Christ must
> have died for all men.

We are confronted with this ambiguous word "all". If the
word means "men of every kind", then we grant the
argument is right. If the word means "the whole human
race", then we deny that God will have them to be saved.

71

The will of God is to be thought of in two ways. There is:

a. His purpose for us – what he wants us to do, and
b. His purpose for himself – what he will do.

Now if God's will in this verse is taken to mean "that which he wants men to do", then the apostle is saying here that God wants the whole human race to use the right means to come to salvation. But a vast proportion of the human race have lived and died without any knowledge of this, for Providence has not taken the means of grace to them! So "all men" can, at best, only mean "all men who have heard the gospel". It cannot possibly mean the whole human race.

If God's will, on the other hand, is taken to mean "that which he intends to do", then we can say that it must have been done. God does whatever he pleases (Psalm 115:3). So if "all men" means the whole human race, then everyone is saved. (If not, then God has failed in his purpose, which is unthinkable).

We do take God's will here to mean "that which he intends to do", and therefore we know it must happen. So we ask: What then can "all men" mean, since, clearly, all men are not saved. By "all men", Paul here means "all sorts of men living in these days of gospel preaching". The means of grace and the boundaries of the church are now extending into all the world. Therefore, we pray for all kinds of people (compare verses 1 and 2 – "kings and those in authority") for the Lord will now save all kinds of people, and not Jews only.

Notice that two things are said:

a. God wills that some of all kinds of men should both be saved and come to a knowledge of the truth.

b.   It is plainly not the will of God that the whole human race should come to a knowledge of the truth, as is clear from scriptures like Psalm 147:19, 20; Matthew 11:25, 26; Acts 14:16; Colossians 1:26; Acts 17:30.

For all these reasons, we deny that "all men" in this scripture can mean the whole human race. It can only mean some men of all sorts who are actually ransomed by Christ – verse 6. This is consistent with what is stated in Revelation 5:9.

2.   Now we come to another scripture often used to suggest a universal atonement – II Peter 3:9. From this verse, it is said:

a.   God does not will any to perish, and

b.   God wills everyone to repent.

Since it is only by Christ's death that men come to repentance, he must have died for everyone.

We need not take many words to answer this. The apostle is speaking here of "us". Who are these? From the context of the letter, we answer – they are those who:

a.   receive great and precious promises – chapter 1:4.

b.   are called "the beloved" – chapter 3:1.

c.   are distinguished from scoffers – chapter 3:3.

d.   are called, in his first letter, "elect" – chapter 1:2.

e.   are called, in his first letter, "purchased people" – chapter 2:9.

Now to argue that because the Lord would have none of these sorts to perish, therefore he wills every man to repent, is surely foolish! The verse clearly means that it is all and only his elect whom he would not have to perish.

3.   The next scripture to examine is Hebrews 2:9. It is

here said that Christ tasted death for everyone. The words "every man" are often used to mean everyone of a certain kind. For example:

a. I Corinthians 12:7 obviously means everyone to whom gifts were actually given.
b. Colossians 1:28 obviously means no more than everyone to whom Paul preached.

So, in this place, the context indicates who those are for whom Christ tasted death. They are (Hebrews 2):

a. many sons (verse 10)
b. the sanctified (verse 11)
c. his brethren (verse 11)
d. children God gave him (verse 13)
e. those who are delivered (verse 15)

It is for everyone of these that Christ has tasted death. Since none of these descriptions can apply to any who remain in unbelief, "every man" here cannot mean the whole human race.

4. II Corinthians 5:14, 15. This is taken to mean that Christ died for all who were dead. But the apostle merely says that all for whom Christ died were dead, and now live to him. Only believers, and all believers, are intended here. Christ is said to die, and rise again, for them. This is only true of believers.

When the apostle says "then were all dead", the death spoken of is not the death of sin in which all men are – a spiritual death; the intention of the apostle is to show that those for whom Christ died are all now dead to sin, and alive instead toward him.

There is nothing here about a universal atonement, but more about Christ's death which results in particular people living a holy life!

74

5. I Corinthians 15:22. That this verse cannot be used to prove that Christ died for all men is clear from the fact that Paul writes, in verse 23, of the resurrection of "they that are Christ's", and in verse 20 of those for whom Christ is "the first fruits". Certainly, these things cannot be said of all men. The apostle speaks here of believers, all of whom died in Adam, and who are all made alive in Christ.

6. Romans 5:18. This is a verse much used by some to support the idea that Christ's death brings life to all men. We might, briefly, say that the "all men" in the second half of the verse can only be understood to mean those on whom the free gift actually comes. They are described in verse 17 as those who "receive abundance of grace", who "reign in life by Jesus Christ"; in verse 19 as those who are "made righteous". Nothing of this can be said of the whole human race.

But since this verse of scripture is so much argued from, we will study the whole passage more fully. It is said that between Christ and Adam there is a resemblance – verse 14. Some things that Christ has done are like some things that Adam did. (At the same time, Paul indicates there are many things different between Adam and Christ – verses 15, 16 and 17. From this we see that we cannot press the likeness between them absolutely.) The comparison here concerns the way that Adam's action affected others as well as himself; so also Christ's action affects others as well as himself. It is not argued that the "all" affected by Adam are the same persons as the "all" affected by Christ. This is made clear by the following:

a.   The scriptures regard Christ as the seed of the woman (Genesis 3:15). It follows therefore that he cannot also be the representative of the seed of the serpent, who are distinguished from the seed of the woman. In other words, Christ cannot represent all Adam's seed or descendants.

b. In John 17:9 Jesus himself indicates that he is not the representative of all men descended from Adam.

c. In Hebrews 7:22, Christ is called the representative of those under a new covenant. This new covenant is not made with all Adam's seed or descendants.

d. From Isaiah 53:5-6 it is clear that Christ was to suffer instead of others. The scriptures indicate that some will suffer for themselves. Therefore Christ is not the representative of all Adam's race.

e. Christ cannot represent anyone in vain. But if he is the representative for all, then his work for the damned is in vain.

f. If God was pleased with what his Son did – as he was – then he must be pleased with all for whom the Son acted. But God is not pleased with all men. Therefore, Christ could not have represented all men.

g. That Christ could not have represented all men, as Adam did, is shown by the plain scriptures: Matthew 20:28; 26:28. John 10:15; 17:9. Acts 20:28. Romans 8:33.

CHAPTER SEVEN

Explanation of those verses which seem to suggest that those for whom Christ died, can still perish

Some argue for a universal redemption on the ground that there are scriptures which suggest that some for whom Christ died, can still perish. In which case, it is no longer a problem that he should die for all, and yet fail to save all.

Let me first say that even if some for whom Christ died are supposedly lost, that does not prove that he died for all who are lost! And, in fact, we deny that any scripture does suggest that any of God's elect can be lost. So let us examine those scriptures so much used by those whom we oppose.

1. Romans 14:15. Here, it is said, Paul teaches that one for whom Christ died, may perish. We answer that no such thing is said. Paul does no more than warn us what not to do. To be warned against a thing does not prove that we can do that thing.

Also, we must remember that scripture uses the terms "saints" and "brethren" to describe all who profess to be members of Christ's church. This passage does not prove that one for whom Christ died can be lost; it can only prove that some we thought of as "brothers" were not really so, if they are eventually lost.

2. I Corinthians 8:11. Here again, it is said, one perishes for whom Christ died. We answer that it is by no means necessary that "perish" in this place means eternal damnation. Sin is always destructive, though it may not always lead to eternal destruction, for some sinners are saved by Christ.

And again, that this one is called "brother" means no more than that he professes to be so. There is no proof here that one for whom Christ died is eternally lost.

3.   II Peter 2:1.   Before this verse can be used to prove that Christ died for all men, including those who perish, it must be shown that:

a.   the Lord Jesus Christ is meant by the term "the Lord",
b.   redemption by the death of Christ is meant by "bought",
c.   these teachers were true believers, and not mere professors,
d.   any of God's elect can perish, and
e.   Christ's death was for all.   .

But these things are all most uncertain, and are no basis for inferring a universal redemption. As we show:

a.   The word used for "Lord" in this place is not the Greek word commonly used for Jesus Christ elsewhere in the New Testament. The word is more applicable to God, as the Master or Owner of all men.
b.   The word "bought" is usually joined with some such words as "with blood" or "by death" or "with a price" when used of Christ's death. The absence of those words here leaves it open, so that what is bought here is merely a general deliverance from some evil of this life – as in verse 20 of this passage.

All that is intended here is that God, in his goodness, preserves some from the worst evils of the world. Yet they, by their false teachings, deny him who preserved them so, and therefore end in destruction. How can anyone prove from this that Christ has died for all men?

4. Hebrews 10:29. Lastly, arguing from this verse, it is said that if any who were sanctified can trample Christ underfoot, then it must mean that he died for them, yet failed to save them. We answer:

a. What is intended here is to show the seriousness of apostasy. It was a serious thing to violate the law of Moses. How much more serious it is to violate the gospel of the Son of God!

b. The persons here referred to, are those professing to be believers. It does not follow that they are truly so.

c. The writer is using a warning to prevent any of his readers from being lost. He says: "If we go on sinning wilfully ..." This does not prove that true believers can go on doing so. In like manner, God warned Joseph to flee into Egypt lest Herod kill the baby Jesus. The warning was given, not because Jesus could be killed (God's purposes were clearly other), but to ensure that he was not.

d. To "be sanctified by the blood of the covenant" does not necessarily prove that these were those for whom Christ died.

   (i) The apostles often addressed churches as "saints", in a collective way. This is no proof that every individual was so.

   (ii) Those who had been baptized were sometimes spoken of as "sanctified", in the sense that they were thereby set-apart from unbaptized persons.

e. If it is insisted that those who trample Christ underfoot are true believers, yet lost, then we have to allow that:

(i) Faith and holiness are not necessarily the marks of God's elect.

(ii) True believers can be separated from Christ.

We have already proved the contrary of both of these.

This passage makes clear to those who merely profess to be Christians how terrible is the sin of ever violating what they profess. And, at the same time, it warns true believers, so that they shall not sin this sin.

And so, with the Lord's assistance, I have given you a clear explanation of the passages of scripture so often used by those who pretend to prove that Christ died for all men, and so I establish our main thesis of Christ's dying only for God's elect.

CHAPTER EIGHT*

Some faulty reasoning exposed

It seems there are some unwise arguments being used these days, which I shall now briefly answer, and so bring this whole work to a close.

1. There is an argument that goes like this:

* Owen has a large section prior to this chapter, in which he deals with the arguments of a book published by one Thomas More, while Owen was writing this "Death of Death". The book: "The Universality of God's Free Grace in Christ to Mankind" is answered in detail by Owen. It seemed unnecessary to include that material here, since that book is not available today.

What everyone is bound to believe, must be true.
Everyone is bound to believe that Christ died for him.
Therefore it is true that Christ died for everyone.

I take it that "everyone" in this argument is to stand for each and every man, and that "believe" is to mean a saving faith in Christ. One thing we do know about all individuals, from scripture, is that they are in a state of spiritual death, and under God's wrath. So the argument is really suggesting that all men, being in a state of death and condemnation, are nevertheless bound to believe that it was God's intention that Christ should die for everyone of them in particular.

Nowhere does the scripture say that Christ died for this or that person in particular, but rather that he died for "sinners", expressed indefinitely. Nor does any command, or promise, of scripture call on any person to believe that Christ died for him in particular.

Also, it cannot be true that each and every man is bound to believe savingly in Christ, unless it can be shown that all have been told to do it. It cannot be the duty of millions who never heard of Christ, to believe savingly in him. Paul shows, in Romans 2:12, that many will be condemned merely for sinning against the light of nature – evidently saving faith in Christ is not required of them!

So the argument must be re-written, to read:

What everyone who is called by the gospel is bound to believe, must be true.
Everyone who hears the gospel is bound to believe Christ died for him in particular.
Therefore it is true that Christ died for everyone who hears the gospel.

Who is there who cannot see that this argument is useless in the cause which it is to defend! We are now admitting that belief is not required of all men, but only of those who actually hear the gospel. So the argument for a universal redemption has already collapsed.

Again, we deny the second proposition. When the gospel is preached, all that can be said is that "he that believes and is baptised shall be saved, but he who disbelieves shall be condemned" (Mark 16:16); or else it can be said that "there is salvation in no-one else; for there is no other name under heaven ... (than that of Christ) ... by which we must be saved" (Acts 4:12). In other words, the duty of the hearers of the gospel is to believe in the necessity of a Saviour, and that Jesus is that Saviour, and not that Christ died for everyone of them in particular.

There is a natural order in the things that God requires to be believed. Until some of them are believed, the rest are not required. A man is not commanded to be at the top of a ladder by skipping all the lower rungs. How opposite it is to the rule of gospel, to call on anyone to believe that Christ died for him in particular, before he is convinced:

(i)   of the truth of the gospel in general,
(ii) that faith is the only way of salvation,
(iii) that he needs a Saviour, and
(iv) that Christ is able to save him.

God's order of things in the believing of the gospel by anyone is, first, to repent and believe that the gospel is the word of God, and that the Jesus revealed there is God's way of salvation; second, that there is an essential connection between faith and salvation; third, a particular conviction, by the Spirit, of the necessity of a Saviour for

82

him in particular, whereby he becomes "weary and heavy laden"; fourth, a serious trusting of the soul to Christ, in response to the promises of the gospel to receive all who thus come to him.

After all this, and not before, there is the assurance of the love of God and the death of Christ for him in particular, based on the fact that he has been enabled to do the first four acts of faith. (For without the help of God's Spirit, none of the former things, much less this last, can be done).

So our argument is to be re-written again:

What everyone who is convinced of the necessity of a Saviour, and of the right way of salvation, hungering and thirsting after Jesus Christ, is bound to believe, must be true.

Every such person is bound to believe that Christ died for him in particular.

Therefore, that Christ did die for such a person, is true.

Now it is clear that not even all who hear the gospel are bound to believe that Christ died for them in particular, but only such of them as are qualified in the way we have described. Failure to believe that Christ died for him in particular is not the cause for any sinner's condemnation. He is condemned already because he has not believed the truth of God's word in general.

So, in order to write this argument in a valid and biblical manner, we have had to progress from the multitudes of the "everyone" (in the first argument) to the "many that are called" (in the first re-writing of the argument) and finally to the "few that are chosen" (in the second re-writing of the argument). Where is there any support here, for a universal redemption?

2.   Another argument used against the teaching that the death of Christ was for the elect alone, is that this doctrine fills the minds of believers with doubts and fears. If Christ did not die for all men, how can they be sure he died for them?

We answer that to know Christ died for him in particular, is not necessary to the sinner's coming to Christ. It is enough if he knows:

a.   that salvation, through Christ's death, is certain to all believers

b.   that he who obeys God's call will certainly be accepted

c.   that free grace is available to all distressed, burdened consciences, and

d.   that Christ's death is adequate for all who come to him.

All this is made certain by the death of Christ. What more is needed? How can such a doctrine as this cause doubts?

On the other hand, if Christ died for all men, and yet some are lost eternallly, then there will be cause for doubts! If *any* for whom Christ died can be damned, then there is no assurance that all may not!

3.   But, say some, surely the grace of God is made so much more glorious if we say that God sent his Son to die for the salvation of all men, if they will but have it.

We answer, what grace of God is it that is to be made universal?

It cannot be the grace of election – for God has not chosen all (Romans 9:11–15)

It cannot be the grace of effectual calling – for God so calls only those he has chosen (Romans 8:30)

It cannot be the grace of sanctification – for only the church is sanctified (Ephesians 5:25–27)

It cannot be the grace of justification – for none but believers are justified (Romans 3:22)

It cannot be the grace of redemption – for the redeemed are taken *out* of every nation (Revelation 5:9)

What grace is it, then, that can be universal?

If it is true that God desires all men saved, on condition they believe, does he not set a condition they cannot fulfil? (As though you offered £100 to a blind man, if he will but open his eyes to see.) How can this magnify God's grace? Does it not rather make him a hypocrite? If you will extend saving grace to all, you extend it to the lost! So a grace that is universal is often ineffectual. Have you really magnified it?

4.   So also, some say the merit of Christ's death is made greater if it is offered for all men.

We answer, the merit of Christ's death is not measured by the number of those to whom it applies, but by whether it achieves what God intended. As long as it does what God intends, it can have no greater merit, whether those who benefit are many or few.

5.   If Christ died for all men, some say, there are greater grounds for all men to draw comfort from his death.

To this we answer, comfort belongs only to believers (Hebrews 6:17, 18); unbelievers are under God's wrath (John 3:36). Believers can gain no comfort by extending the death of Christ to include those who remain under the wrath of God.

In any time of trial and temptation, let a man try to comfort himself with the argument:

> Christ died for all men;
> I am a man;
> Therefore Christ died for me.

Will not his own heart tell him this is false reasoning? Are there not millions of the sons of men to whom God does not reveal himself? What comfort is there in this?

A great source of comfort, to the believer, is the fact that Christ now intercedes for those for whom he died. This we have shown before (Part One, Chapter Seven). Now if Christ's death is for all men, his intercession plainly is not (John 17:9). So Christ's death, if separated from his intercession, is no longer a sense of comfort. We have not increased our comfort by enlarging the atonement of his death wider than his intercession.

If the faith and holiness of the elect are not obtained for them by the death of Christ, where have they come from? They can only have come from themselves! Is this the enlarged comfort you offer, to send us away from God's free grace, to our "free" will? Where will you send the soul that desires faith and holiness? Do you not send him to God, who gives all freely, through Christ's obtaining of them?

But, so it is said, no-one can be sure Christ died for him, unless Christ died for everyone.

We answer: This must be quite wrong, since many believers *are* sure Christ died for them, though they do not believe he died for all men! The basis of assurance is the fact that Christ died for all believers. Not that he died for them because they believe; but that they believe because he died for them. He died for the elect, who by the benefit of his death, become believers. They know, by the work of the Spirit in them, that they have sincerely come to Christ for mercy. They know that scripture declares that the death of Christ is sufficient for everyone who thus comes to him. And since they find themselves believers, they may know that Christ has died for them.

Now let the reader judge for himself, is not this a better basis for assurance than the false argument:

> Christ died for all men (including the lost);
> I am a man;
> Therefore he died for me?

For a closing argument, let the reader study Romans 8:32-34. I have no doubt that he will then conclude that any spiritual comfort to be obtained is only in the blood of Jesus long since shed, and in his intercession still continued, both being for the elect of God, to the obtaining of an immortal crown of glory that cannot fade away.

GREAT CHRISTIAN CLASSICS SERIES

Easier-to-read and abridged versions of Christian classics.

No.1 LIFE BY HIS DEATH

Prepared by H. J. Appleby
John Owen's **The Death of Death in the Death of Christ.**
Paperback, 87 pages. ISBN 0 9505476 3 8.
' ... *a brilliant abridgement. The whole church of Christ stands in debt to John Appleby for undertaking this work.'*

Stuart Olyott

No.2 GOD WILLING

Prepared by H. Mockford
John Flavel's **Divine Conduct or The Mystery of Providence.**
Paperback, 65 pages. ISBN 0 9505476 6 2.
'This volume borders on the masterly ... You must buy it and read it again and again.'

Evangelical Magazine of Wales

No.3 BIBLICAL CHRISTIANITY

Prepared by B. R. Woods
John Calvin's **The Institutes of the Christian Religion.**
Paperback, 125 pages. ISBN 0 9505476 7 0.
'This is an excellent little book. It deserves a worldwide circulation!'

Evangelical Times

No.4 BY GOD'S GRACE ALONE

Prepared by H. J. Appleby
Abraham Booth's **The Reign of Grace.**
Paperback, 73 pages. ISBN 0 946462 01 1.
'One does not doubt that Mr Appleby has made a sound job of this rendering ...'

Gospel Magazine

NO.5 BORN SLAVES

Prepared by Clifford Pond
Martin Luther's **The Bondage of the Will.**
Paperback, 93 pages. ISBN 0 946462 02 X.
'This excellent, easy to read edition of Luther's book will help us to think clearly about a subject which has often been the source of such confusion.'

Fellowship Magazine

No.6 THE GLORY OF CHRIST

Prepared by H. Mockford
John Owen's **The Glory of Christ.**
Paperback, 86 pages. ISBN 0 946462 13 5.

No.7 CHRISTIANS ARE FOR EVER!

Prepared by H. Lawrence
John Owen's **The Perseverance of the Saints.**
Paperback, 84 pages. ISBN 0 946462 14 3.

No.8 LEARNING TO BE HAPPY

Prepared by Philip Tait and Sharon James
Jeremiah Burrough's **The Rare Jewel of Christian Contentment.**
Paperback, 64 pages. ISBN 0 946462 16 X.
'This book can be recommended particularly for use with ... the young Christian of any age.'

Peace and Truth

No.9 THINKING SPIRITUALLY

Prepared by John Appleby and Philip Grist
John Owen's **The Grace and Duty of being Spiritually Minded.**
Paperback, 96 pages. ISBN 0 946462 21 6.
'I found this book both challenging and delightful'

Presbyterian Banner

No.10 NOT GUILTY

Prepared by John Appleby
James Buchanan's **Justification.**
Paperback, 96 pages. ISBN 0 946462 22 4.
' ... eminently readable'

Living Today

No.11 THE EXPERIENCE THAT COUNTS

Prepared by N. R. Needham
Jonathan Edwards' **Treatise concerning Religious Affections.**
Paperback, 128 pages. ISBN 0 964642 23 2.
'This book is very deep, but very simple and will suit all ages.'
The Gospel Magazine

GATEWAY SERIES

Simplified versions of Christian classics.

WHO IS IN CONTROL?

Prepared by R. Devenish
A simplification of the substance of A. W. Pink's **The Sovereignty of God.**
Paperback, 58 pages. ISBN 9505476 4 6.

INTO LIFE

Prepared by R. Devenish
A simplification of the substance of **The Rise and Progress of Religion in the Soul** by Philip Doddridge.
Paperback, 59 pages. ISBN 9505476 5 4.

POPULAR PAPERBACKS

NO LOOKING BACK
The story of a Missionary to India

David Thrower
Based on David Thrower's memories and diaries, this book is an account of over sixty years working among the Tamil people of India, proclaiming the good news of Jesus Christ.
Paperback, 160 pages. ISBN 0 946462 08 9.

INTERPRETING THE BIBLE

W. N. H. Kuhrt
The author has set out clear guidelines for the proper interpretation of God's Word. By following the principles that are set out the Bible student will be enabled to understand the message of the Bible with greater clarity. This is no technical handbook for the expert but a tool suited to every Bible reader.
Paperback, 106 pages. ISBN 9505476 8 9.

C. H. SPURGEON AND THE MODERN CHURCH

Robert Sheehan
During Spurgeon's lifetime the influx of modernism led to virtually all the major doctrines of historic Christianity being denied. The author sketches Spurgeon's stand against this and outlines the principles that dominated his thinking. At a time when modernism dominates all the major denominations, it is necessary to consider again Spurgeon's historic stand.
Paperback, 124 pages. ISBN 0 946462 05 4.

GOD'S PLAN FOR THE LOCAL CHURCH

Nigel Lacey
What can we learn from Scripture about the life and practice of the local church? In covering such issues as the nature and glory of the church, its membership, discipline and government and inter-church relationships, Nigel Lacey challenges the reader to learn afresh of God's purposes for his church.
Paperback, 124 pages. ISBN 0 946462 07 0.
'Here is pure gold.'

Church Weekly Newspaper

I WANT TO BE BAPTISED

Eric Lane
Here is an ideal, practical book to use with candidates thinking about, or preparing for baptism. Eric Lane takes the reader through the Bible's teaching on the ordinance with a special view to the personal commitment involved. Excellent for use as a basis for study groups or for personal reading.
Paperback, 128 pages. ISBN 0 946462 08 9.
'Eric Lane's purpose in writing this book is to bring out what could be termed the sanctifying influence of baptism for the believer ... I warmly commend this book ... It deserves a wide circulation.'

David Kingdon

WE BELIEVE

Grace Baptist Assembly
This publication comprises two historic documents, 'The Baptist Affirmation of Faith 1966' and 'A Guide to Church Fellowship'.
Paperback, 105 pages. ISBN 0 946462 00 3.

ONLY SERVANTS ...
A view of the place, responsibilities and ministries of elders in local churches

Clifford Pond

Clifford Pond writes out of a lifetime of pastoral ministry, having served churches in Suffolk and Surrey as well as exercising a wider ministry at various times by responsible leadership in young people's fellowships, associations of churches and the council of Grace Baptist Mission.

Now in retirement, Clifford writes in a warm, friendly style which well reflects the personal nature of the experiences that he has gained over the years, in which he has helped churches to develop in New Testament maturity.

He has not shirked difficult aspects of the establishment of elderships in churches, but has sought to offer a careful and balanced discussion of them for the help of 'ordinary believers'. Large paperback, 176 pages. ISBN 0 946462 24 0.